Travel and Teach the World

Great Schools, Great Pay and a Great Life as an International School Teacher

By:

Philip Gill

Copyright © 2014 Philip Gill

All rights reserved.

ISBN: 1505638240

ISBN-13: 978-1505638240

DEDICATION

To all the great people I had the opportunity to get to know in my journeys to Japan, China, Egypt, and the United States. In particular, I'd like to thank Cathy Spencer. Without her encouragement and mentorship, I would have not written this book.

Contents

Preface - Teacher Certification and International Teaching 1
   Teaching ESL Abroad 2
   Teaching Certification 4

Part I: Is This the Life for You? 7
   International Schools 9
   Is Teaching at an International School Right for You? 11
   Where Will You Go? 15
   Regions of the World 17
      Western Europe 17
      Eastern Europe 18
      Latin America 18
      The Middle East and North Africa 19
      East Asia 20
      South-East Asia 21
      Sub-Saharan Africa 21
   Making the Decision to Teach at an International School . 22

Part II - Becoming an International School Teacher: Defining Your Candidacy 25
   What You'll Need to Do Once You've Made Your Decision 26
   Things That Make You Stand Out to Recruiters 30
      International Experience 30
      A Background in Coaching, Music, or Theatre 32

Ability and Willingness to Teach More than One Subject 33

Familiarity with The International Baccalaureate (IB) Program 34

Part III - Becoming an International School Teacher: Strategies for Your Job Search 35

Types of International Schools and Programs 36

British and American Schools 36

IB Schools 36

Non-Profit vs. For-Profit Schools 37

Department of Defense Educational Activity Schools ... 39

The Fulbright Teacher Exchange Program 40

Search Strategies 40

The Winter Recruiting Strategy – Peak Season 42

The Late Season Strategy: Round II of Recruiting and the Month of June 49

Which Strategy Should You Use? 52

Accepting a Job 59

Problems That You Might Run into When You're Teaching Abroad 61

Part IV - Benefits and Salaries 65

Benefits 66

Housing 66

Health Insurance 67

Airfares 68

Tuition for Dependent Children 68

Assistance with Visas 69
  Taxes 69
 Salaries at International Schools 70

Part V - Relationship Status and How it Can Affect Your Job Search 73

  Relationship Status 74
    Single Teachers 74
    Teaching Couples 75
    Teachers with a Non-Teaching Spouse 76
    Children 77
    Pet Ownership 77

Part VI - Websites, Recruiting Agencies, and Other Resources for International School Teaching Candidates 79

  Essential Websites 80
    Times Educational Supplement (TES) 80
    International Schools Review (ISR) 81
    The International Educator (TIE) 83
  Recruiting Agencies and Hiring Fairs 84
    Registration with a Recruiting Agency 84
    Attending a Hiring Fair 85
  The Recruiting Agencies 88
    Search Associates 88
    International Schools Services (ISS) 89
    University of Northern Iowa Overseas Placement Service 90

The Association of American Schools in South America (AASSA) 91

Council of International Schools (CIS) 91

Teachers' Overseas Recruiting Fair (TORF) 92

Part VII - Final Words and a Directory of Some Well Known International Schools 93

Final Words 94

Some of the Better-Known International Schools 95

Preface:

Teacher Certification and International Teaching
Teaching ESL Abroad vs. Teaching at an International School

Teaching ESL Abroad

Teaching abroad is a great way to see the world, and there are many options available for people who are considering this path. The easiest one is probably to teach English as a Second Language or ESL. Depending on which country you go to, you can get a job teaching ESL with a certificate in ESL teaching which can be earned in just a few weeks or with even less.

Some ESL schools will hire teachers with just a college degree. Some teachers can get hired without one. However, to be considered fully qualified to teach ESL abroad, it is probably the best idea to first earn a TESOL certificate. TESOL certificates can be earned online in a short amount of time for just a few hundred dollars. If you are serious about working abroad, it is a very good idea to be prepared before you make the commitment. Spending a few hundred dollars and a couple of months before you go abroad can greatly expand your teaching opportunities and give you much more flexibility in your job search.

Teaching ESL abroad provides one with a great deal of flexibility. It is possible to travel from country to country spending a few months in each one, while making enough money to fund your trip. ESL schools may expect a teacher to sign a contract to teach for a year, but this isn't always the case. In general, a teacher can work for a school for a relatively short period of time and then move on to another school in another country.

The salary and benefits can vary greatly for teachers who teach ESL abroad. The very best jobs are generally filled by teachers who have an advanced degree in teaching ESL, but there are plenty of excellent jobs available to teachers with a college degree and an ESL certificate.

For people who are interested in teaching abroad immediately and are not certified to teach primary school or secondary school, teaching ESL is probably the right choice, but if you are certified or you are willing to get certified to teach in a primary or secondary school, there are many high quality jobs that pay significantly better than ESL jobs. There are jobs available for teachers who are looking to start a career teaching abroad. Most international schools welcome teachers who plan on staying for a long time.

Teaching Certification

A teaching certificate is the primary qualification you'll need to teach at an international school. Although it is not impossible to get hired to teach at an international school without a teaching certificate, a teaching certificate will greatly expand your options.

Unlike TESOL certificates, teaching certificates are issued by states and countries. Naturally to teach at an international school, the certification to have is one from the US, the UK or from other countries where English is the first language.

If you would like to teach at an international school, and you are not yet certified to teach, it is possible to earn a certificate relatively quickly, but in the US this varies from state to state. The website certificationmap.com provides links to the requirements for each state. Naturally it is far easier to earn a teaching certificate in some states than in other states, but when earning your certificate be sure that you'll be able to use it when you return home. Although many states accept teaching certificates that were earned in other states, this is not always the case. Also, states often change their requirements, and what works now might not work a few years from now when you return from teaching abroad. Make sure you do your research if you are considering becoming certified by a state where you're not planning on living when you return from teaching abroad.

Once you are certified to teach, it is time to ask yourself the big question. Is international teaching right for you?

Part I

Is This the Life for You?
Introduction to International Schools and the Life of International School Teachers

Teaching at an international school is a great opportunity for a teacher in the English-speaking world who is interested in travel and in truly experiencing a new culture for an extended period of time. In many ways it's the perfect job. You'll live abroad for ten months of the year, and during the breaks from school you'll be able to return home and travel the world. You'll meet students and teachers from all over the world. You'll have a chance to learn a new language, try new foods, and learn new things about the world and about yourself.

In other ways the job is less than perfect. You'll leave your friends, family, and country, and enter a world of unfamiliarity.

After you sign your first contract to teach abroad, the days and months will rush by, and before you know it, you'll be saying goodbye to your previous life and hello to your new one. But before you do, there are many steps you'll need to take. There are many questions you'll need to ask yourself and your potential employers before committing to your time abroad. Teaching at an international school is not a decision that should be taken lightly. There are many things that you'll need to consider, and it's important that you take the right steps.

International Schools

Just a few decades ago, there were only a few schools outside of the English-speaking world where Western trained teachers were able to get jobs teaching their subjects in foreign countries. Students in these schools were generally the children of diplomats, foreign military personnel, and expatriate employees of corporations.

The target market for these schools was almost exclusively expatriates. These schools still exist today, and it's very likely that these are some of the international schools you'll be applying to once you begin your job search. Many of the better known international schools have been around for the better part of a century, but these days there are far more international schools than there once were.

Recently international education has become a booming growth industry where local students have joined in and have greatly increased their presence at the schools. Currently there are well over 5000 English Language international schools worldwide.

Why the rapid growth? In many countries, it is expected that members of the upper and middle classes speak native or near native level English. Families in these countries recognize the importance of building these language skills at an early age and seek out the truly immersive environment that international schools offer. This means that when you move abroad, you are very likely to find yourself teaching a larger proportion of local students than you ever would have before, as the popularity of international schools increases worldwide among local populations.

This has happened to such a degree that some schools, although referred to as international schools and staffed by foreign teachers, are attended exclusively, or almost exclusively, by local students, and this trend is continuing. This means that for qualified teachers, there are opportunities to be found in increasing numbers worldwide since every year there are more international schools than ever before.

Also at the moment there are more teachers than ever before who are interested in working at these schools. With poor economic conditions in much of the English-speaking world and plenty of teachers unable to find jobs or make a good living teaching in their own countries, many teachers are looking abroad for better opportunities. Nevertheless, for teachers who are prepared to start teaching abroad, a buyer's market awaits.

The landscape can seem overwhelming and is at times, and at some schools it's highly competitive to get a job teaching. However, with the right attitude and the right approach, you can get hired as a teacher at an international school and have the opportunity to explore a new culture, travel the world, and have an experience most can only dream of.

In addition, many international schools offer packages that allow teachers to live lifestyles far beyond the ones they have in the West. Large apartments usually come paid for with teaching contracts. Maids, drivers, and personal chefs are far more affordable in most parts of the world than you're probably used to, and it is normal for teachers at international schools to employ them in addition to saving significant parts of their salaries.

Is Teaching at an International School Right for You?

This is a very important question to ask yourself. If you are considering teaching abroad for the first time, you are not considering a standard career change. Rather, you are considering a life-transforming experience. Think about all that you hold dear where you live now. Consider your family, your friends, your favorite stores, your favorite sights, and even the smells. How will it affect you when all of these are 10,000 kilometers away and inaccessible until December or June? Is it realistic for you to give up your job, give up your apartment, sell your things (or pay to put them in storage), and say goodbye to your family and friends? How attached are you to your own culture and to your current routines? When you move abroad, you'll quickly notice that things are done in a manner that's quite different from the way you would expect them to be done if you were at home. If you've traveled extensively, you've undoubtedly noticed that there are some things that may be done more efficiently or handled more appropriately than they are in your home country. Surely you've also noticed that some things are done less efficiently and are handled in ways that are worse than you are used to.

Unfortunately, it is sometimes the latter that people dwell on when they're living abroad. Clothes in stores might be sized differently than you're used to. You might not be able to find your favorite foods, or they may be expensive or hard to get. If you move to Asia, the food will be drastically different from what you're used to. If you move to certain countries, you might have trouble finding alcohol or pork. Even if you can get the things you are used to, you might not be able to get the varieties you like. You may have to get accustomed to a large number of inconvenient things, from drivers who don't obey traffic lights to not being able to flush away toilet paper. These differences will be noticeable when you relocate, and they will be a part of your everyday life. However, when living abroad it is very important to try to focus on the positive differences. Dwelling too much on the things you don't like about your new country will lead to a less than ideal experience.

This cultural question is important for several reasons, primarily because you have to be sure you are making the right decision before you commit to a teaching position for the following year or two. Once you've moved into an apartment in a foreign country, it's too late to reconsider your decision, without serious consequences. Once you've signed a contract to teach abroad for the next school year, it can be problematic if you renege on your promise, and the terms of some international school contracts dictate that if you don't complete your contract, you'll be held financially liable for the school's costs to hire you. International schools invest significant sums of money recruiting teachers, and once a teacher signs a contract for the following year, the school begins processing paperwork to ensure that the teacher will be allowed to work in the country when the school year begins. This process is time-consuming and can be very costly for the school.

Also, one broken contract can make it more difficult for a teacher to get another job at an international school in the future.

International school recruiters understand that moving abroad and the culture shock associated with this can have serious effects on a teacher. It can lower performance, and it can lead to unfinished contracts. When teachers don't finish contracts, it puts a great deal of strain on international school administrators. It can be very difficult, not to mention costly, to find a replacement teacher in the middle of the year. Because of this, recruiters will make their own judgments regarding how suitable you are as a candidate. If they sense that you have any doubt about your decision to teach abroad, they will be very unlikely to hire you.

If you are considering teaching abroad, take some time to make your decision. Be honest with yourself. It is not right for everyone. But if you decide that it is for you, make the decision with confidence, and let this confidence guide you through the search and interview process. This will allow you to seek out and find the international teaching jobs that are right for you. It will allow you to excel at your interviews, and with it you will take on the challenge that will show you the world in a way you've never seen it before.

Where Will You Go?

The answer to this question is not so simple. Maybe you have already made a decision about where you'd like to teach. If you are only interested in one or even two countries, realize that you are greatly limiting your possibilities to the point that you will probably not get the job you are after. As is undoubtedly the case with schools where you live, international schools are already staffed with teachers, and every year a few teachers may leave. Then the schools search for teachers to fill vacancies.

If a teacher, rather than looking broadly for where those vacancies are, chooses just one school or just a few schools, the chances are quite slim of getting hired anywhere. In many countries, there are only a handful of international schools. If you just target these, it's not likely that you'll be hired. Consider first whether or not these few schools are actually hiring anyone who teaches your subject. Even if the answer is yes and there's a posting for a job in your license area, often it will still not be possible to get the job. Maybe that school requires very specific qualifications or specific experience that you don't have.

Even if you are the perfect candidate for the position, realize that, with the time constraints and with the volume of recruiting that international schools do, recruiters will aggressively hire candidates who are qualified to fill teaching positions, often on the spot. In the world of international schools it is not uncommon for schools to cancel interviews with candidates because they have hired someone who was lucky enough to be interviewed first. It is not uncommon at hiring fairs for a candidate to see that dream job crossed off the list of openings, while waiting in line to inquire about it.

Because of these factors, the best way to ensure you'll get a job at an international school is to be flexible about where you'll go. There are so many opportunities out there for teachers who are willing to go somewhere unfamiliar, and if you expand you range of possibilities, the ease in finding a job will greatly increase. It is generally suggested that you be open to at least two general regions of the world.

The more open and the more flexible you are, the more likely you'll be to find a job, and the more choices you'll have.

Regions of the World

It's important to consider the pros and cons of different regions of the world when you're choosing ones where you may live. Try to pick at least two broad regions from these.

Western Europe

Western Europe has some great places to live. The lifestyle and the culture are outstanding. Some schools in Western Europe even offer very generous salaries, but very few include housing as a part of their packages. Add to this some of the highest taxes and highest costs of living in the world, and your money will not go far as a teacher in Western Europe.

Also, International school teachers compete fiercely for jobs teaching in Western Europe. As a teacher new to international schools, you may be better off focusing on other regions of the world.

Eastern Europe

Countries in Eastern Europe generally offer moderate to high salaries, along with low taxes and a relatively low cost of living. The schools are usually less competitive in terms of their hiring than schools in Western Europe, but this depends a lot on the country and on the school. Eastern Europe has much of the culture and beauty that Western Europe has, but it should be possible to live much better here on a teacher's salary.

Latin America

In South America, the top schools in the richer countries have some of the highest salaries and the best packages in the world, while schools in the poorer countries have among the lowest salaries you'll find anywhere. Schools in the more developed countries like Brazil, Chile, and Argentina generally offer better salaries and packages than schools in the less developed countries in the region such as Bolivia, Ecuador, and Belize.

Venezuela is considered a hardship post because of the political situation, but the country has a tremendous amount of oil wealth. This is reflected in the generous packages offered by international schools here.

The cost of living is quite low in Mexico and the salaries, although not the best internationally, will go quite far in this country.

The countries in Central America and the Caribbean have lower costs of living than many others and are highly desirable places to work. Schools in this region seem to be well aware that they can pay teachers less than schools in other countries and still have overflowing inboxes whenever a job is posted because of the popularity of this region among international school teachers.

In general, the low cost of living in Latin America makes it an attractive region to teach in.

The Middle East and North Africa

The Middle East and North Africa make up a high growth area when it comes to international schools. New schools are opening regularly. Culturally, some countries, particularly Saudi Arabia, are very restrictive while others, such as Lebanon, are much more open. The salaries and benefit packages at many schools in this region are some of the best in the world. The cost of living is generally quite low with the exception of some of the Gulf States and Lebanon.

Be careful with this region. Because of the rapid growth in demand for international education, new schools of varying quality open all the time. Research the schools you are interested in to make sure they are high quality before you sign a contract with an unfamiliar school here.

East Asia

In China, there are many schools of varying quality. You'll find some of the best and highest paying schools in the world along with some of the worst fly-by-night operations. If you work at a good school in China, you'll benefit from a low cost of living relative to the salary you receive.

Korean schools also pay quite well, the cost of living is reasonable, and there are several well-established international schools in Korea. In China and Korea, new schools are opening all the time because of the rapid growth the industry is seeing, and just like in the Middle East, you'll need to be careful and do your research before accepting a position in this region.

Schools in Japan, with the country's high economic status, generally offer very good packages to compensate somewhat for the country's high cost of living.

South-East Asia

There is very high demand for an international education in South-East Asia as well, and most countries have quite a few international schools. Schools in the wealthier countries in the region can offer great packages, and many countries in this region also have a very low cost of living. South-East Asia, with the possible exception of Singapore and Hong Kong, is one of those regions where teachers can make their salaries go very far.

Be cautious here just as you would in East Asia and the Middle East. This is a high growth region with schools of varying quality.

Sub-Saharan Africa

With the exception of a few schools in some of the larger, more developed cities, schools in Sub-Saharan Africa pay salaries that are quite low. Expenses are quite low as well, so in this region you should be able to live reasonably well and save a good part of your salary.

In many cases, once you're outside of the major cities in Sub-Saharan Africa, there is not much to spend money on in the way of imports and the general variety of goods available.

Making the Decision to Teach at an International School

Be sure to discuss the decision to teach at an international school with your family and your friends. Take some time to consider whether or not this is really for you. Ask yourself the question, "Am I ready to begin a search for a job at an international school that will end with my signing a contract and teaching abroad for two years?" Once you can enthusiastically answer yes to this question, momentum will guide you through the steps that will lead to your living in some part of the world that you had previously only dreamed of.

Understand that by answering yes to this question you are committing yourself to a period of at least one year, more likely two years working abroad. The point here is that because of the recruiting atmosphere among international schools, once you decide that this is for you, it's almost as if you've already accepted a job abroad.

But before you make a final decision, it's OK to try to get an idea of what's involved. Subscribe to a website or two that provides information. Read through some job postings. You may even feel compelled to send off your resume to a few school recruiters. However, this is a major decision, and if you are not yet committed to the move, it's not a good idea to pursue it too far. Also recruiters will likely recognize it if you haven't yet defined yourself as a candidate, so it will be clear to them that you haven't yet made the decision to teach abroad.

Part II

Becoming an International School Teacher: Defining Your Candidacy

This section describes what you'll need to do to define yourself as a candidate in a way that recruiters expect and in a way that will greatly improve your chances of getting the right job teaching abroad.

What You'll Need to Do Once You've Made Your Decision

The international school community is rather fluid. Teachers and administrators move from school to school and from country to country. Because of this, there is some uniformity in the way these schools recruit teachers and in what recruiters expect from candidates. One of the most obvious examples of this is the way candidates are defined. Before you're able to target schools that you want to get hired by, you'll need to define yourself as a candidate. You may notice that some of the steps are time consuming. Recruiters like to see that candidates have put in a significant amount of time and effort defining their candidacy. This assures recruiters that they are dealing with candidates who are serious about working abroad.

Begin taking these steps as soon as you've made your decision.

Prepare your resume. Make sure it emphasizes your teaching experience, your international experience, and is written to a high standard. If you haven't searched for a job in a while, it is likely that your resume needs some major revisions or even a complete rewrite. There are many resources (books and websites) that provide formats for resumes. Choose a format that will best reflect your strengths and distinguish you from the competition. Be sure you have someone look over your resume to ensure it's consistent in format and free of errors. You might even want to hire someone to work with you on perfecting it. It's very easy to fall into a trap with a resume where it says what you think it should say but doesn't say what the people who would hire you want to hear. Make sure you aim it at the reader.

If you are currently teaching, inform your principal that you are planning on searching for a job at an international school. This may be one of the most difficult steps. You are essentially announcing that you are planning on resigning. You may worry that your decision will be taken badly. Try to be open and describe how and why you came to your decision. Try to make sure the meeting ends on a positive tone and that you have the support of your principal. You'll need it, because you should have a letter of recommendation from your current principal, and schools that are interested in hiring you will very likely want to speak with your current and past supervisors. If you are not currently teaching, you'll need to get in touch with your most recent supervisor.

Prepare to have at least three letters of recommendation written for you. One should be from your current principal, and there is some flexibility regarding the two others. If you've been in the habit of getting letters from all your previous supervisors, you can naturally use these, but if you haven't you'll need to get in touch with them. One of the best ways to get a letter of recommendation is to accompany your request with an electronic document with bullet points that cover your achievements. Don't expect your principal to remember all of the great things you've done. If you don't give your principal something to work with, depending on how much time your principal has, you may end up with a generic letter that doesn't really say much about what you've achieved. A bulleted list will make your letter writers' jobs much easier, and it will get you letters that you can better incorporate into your job search strategy. Also be sure to inform the people who write letters for you that they may also be asked to write confidential references for you in the future. Some recruiting organizations require you to have confidential references on file in order to register with them.

Begin formulating an individual search strategy that takes into account your experience and objectives. Start reviewing some job listings. Sign up for *The International Educator* (www.tieonline.com) and start reviewing their job postings and reading their magazine. Consider signing up with a recruiting agency. These are discussed in depth in Part VI. Regularly review the postings in the *Times of London* (www.tes.co.uk) Educational Supplement. Become familiar with several websites of international schools that you are interested in. Get to know what jobs are out there and what qualifications are expected. Think about what geographical regions you're interested in working in. Try to pick at least two broad ones. Make a list of your desires. What are your first choices in terms of specific schools? What are a few cities where you would most like to end up? Begin your search with these places. Also consider if there are any places where you would definitely not want to move to. Defining all these things before you start searching seriously will make your search much more efficient and effective.

Things That Make You Stand Out to Recruiters

You'll need to ensure that recruiters are interested in you. In general international schools require teachers they hire to be officially licensed to teach by a recognized licensing body in their country of origin. In addition to this, schools look for teachers that have at least two years of full-time teaching experience in their subject areas. In many countries these requirements are firm, because their immigration bureaus will not grant work visas to teachers who don't meet these requirements. However, this is not always the case. Some of the less prestigious international schools are willing to hire teachers with little or no teaching experience. Some will even hire teachers who aren't licensed.

Beyond these requirements, there are many other things that recruiters look for when they are reviewing applications from prospective teachers.

International Experience

Naturally, experience teaching at an international school will put you ahead of teachers who don't have it. In the eyes of international school recruiters, the best type of experience is teaching experience in your subject at an international school in a country that's foreign to you. Not everyone is cut out for this type of work, so if you've done it before, you'll stand out.

Experience teaching English as a Second Language abroad is good as well. It's quite different from subject teaching in a high school or elementary school setting, but it will demonstrate that you are comfortable working abroad. Therefore recruiters will feel that they are taking less of a risk than hiring someone with no international work experience at all.

Study abroad programs may not distinguish you like international work experience, but they will show a recruiter that you have international awareness and should be able to adapt. Even extensive travel experience can set you apart from candidates who have not been exposed to foreign cultures.

What if You Have No Significant International Experience?

Is international experience really necessary? International school recruiters look for international experience for a reason. Some people aren't able to handle the changes that they encounter when they leave their countries. If you haven't spent much time abroad, take some steps to determine if this decision is really right for you. It is possible to get international experience by volunteering abroad. International GoAbroad.com has a database of international volunteer opportunities (www.goabroad.com/volunteer-abroad). Many of them are available for a summer and may be appropriate for you to experience just before you start your job search.

It is also possible to rent an apartment abroad for a summer and enroll in a language school in a foreign country. By doing this you'll be immersed in a foreign culture, you'll meet plenty of people who are not from your country, and you'll be able to decide for yourself whether or not international living is right for you. These types of experiences will define you as a more serious candidate in the eyes of recruiters than if you've had no international experience. Be sure you note them on your resume.

A Background in Coaching, Music, or Theatre

Other experience can be beneficial as well. Among international schools there is a significant amount of competition. Students and their parents are attracted to schools that they consider to be the best. Being the best can mean many different things. It can mean being ranked very high academically. It can also mean having a team that regularly wins regional championships. It can also mean putting on the best plays or concerts.

Teachers who have experience coaching or directing musical or theatrical productions should emphasize this in their resumes and in correspondence with recruiters.

Even experience playing a sport or working in music or in theatre, along with a willingness to contribute to these programs can make a big difference. Being able to contribute in one of these areas will often turn an otherwise average candidate into an exceptional one.

Ability and Willingness to Teach More than One Subject

Can you teach more than one subject? International schools try to offer a broad range of courses, even when they are small. Often it is more efficient for a school to hire teachers who can move between two subjects rather than having to hire teachers who can only teach one. It gives the administration more flexibility with scheduling and shows that you are a flexible teacher.

Familiarity with The International Baccalaureate (IB) Program

The IB is very popular among international schools. Schools that offer IB programs generally seek teachers who have experience teaching it, and experience teaching in the IB program will make it much easier to get a job at a school that offers it. Details about the IB can be found at www.ibo.org.

If you plan on teaching internationally for a while, it is a very good idea to get IB experience if you can. Teachers with IB experience are in high demand, because there is a shortage of them.

You could even boost your chances of getting hired if you can demonstrate that you are actually familiar with the program and the content that you'd be expected to teach in an IB program. Research the IB courses that you're able to teach, so you can discuss them in you correspondence and in interviews.

Part III

Becoming an International School Teacher: Strategies for Your Job Search

Before beginning to seriously search for a job teaching at an international school, it is important that you know what types of schools you'll be applying to.

Types of International Schools and Programs

British and American Schools

There are two main types of English speaking international schools. These are schools that use an American style curriculum and schools that use a British one. American schools favor teachers who have experience teaching the American curriculum up through AP courses in high school. British schools favor teachers who have experience teaching the British national curriculum. This includes the GCSEs and A-Level courses in secondary school. Because of this, it will be more difficult for you to get a job in a British school if you are only experienced working in American schools and vice-versa.

IB Schools

In addition to British and American schools, there are IB schools. IB schools follow a special curriculum that is set by the International Baccalaureate Organization. Many schools offer IB programs alongside an American or British curriculum. Schools can subscribe to the Primary Years Program (PYP), the Middle Years Program (MYP), and the Diploma Program (DP). IB training is available, and schools often send teachers to be trained before they teach their first IB courses. If you get hired by a school that offers the IB, discuss the possibility of teaching IB courses with an administrator. Most teachers do not have experience teaching IB, and this experience can really set you apart when you look for your next job internationally.

Non-Profit vs. For-Profit Schools

As is the case in the West, many private schools are run as non-profit organizations, while others are run as businesses. In theory non-profit schools should be better places to work. There are no shareholders, and income that's left over after expenses goes into improvement of the school or into the school's endowment for later use.

In for-profit schools, there are shareholders who are looking for returns on their investment. This means that at least part of the income left over after expenses goes to these investors.

What all this means is that if you get a job at a for-profit international school, there may be efforts made to minimize expenses in favor of increasing profits. However, there are many for-profit schools that are very well run and have programs that are well-funded. There are also non-profit schools that are poorly run and are not adequately resourced.

When looking for a teaching position, be aware that the budgets at for-profit schools may be thinner relative to their revenues than at non-profit schools. If you are concerned about working at one of these schools, do some research, and make an effort to talk to teachers currently working at the school. Try to address any concerns you have before signing a contract. But don't just assume that a non-profit school will always be a better place to work than a for-profit school. In general it is always good to research individual schools while keeping in mind what the financial goals are at each type of school.

Also, the rapid growth that's going on with international schools is primarily in the for-profit sector. Currently and in the future, you can expect that it will be in the for-profit schools where the majority of opportunities are.

Department of Defense Educational Activity Schools

If you'd like to live abroad in an American environment, dealing with the children of American military personnel and children of Department of Defense civilian employees, these schools are a great option. They offer great salaries and can include the shipment of an automobile and a very large quantity of household goods among the perks. If you are hired by a Department of Defense school, you'll travel on an official passport and have all the benefits that embassy employees and military personnel have when you're abroad working. You'll be able to shop at the commissary and ship goods to the US at domestic rates.

In many subject areas, these schools are quite competitive, and the amount of paperwork you'll need to go through to get hired by one is significant. If this kind of work appeals to you, more information is available on the Department of Defense Educational Activity Schools website (http://www.dodea.edu/offices/hr/default.htm), where you'll find information on requirements, vacancies, salaries, benefits, and much more information about these schools.

The Fulbright Teacher Exchange Program

For qualified American teachers, the Bureau of Educational and Cultural Affairs at the United States Department of State offers an exchange program that allows teachers to go abroad for one year (extendable to two) and exchange jobs and apartments with a teacher in a foreign country while continuing to be paid by your school at home.

On the surface this is a great opportunity. The problem is that many teachers have reported being accepted to the program but not actually being placed in a school abroad. You'll need to interview to get accepted, but actual placements abroad are rare. You can find more information about the Fulbright program here:

http://www.fulbrightteacherexchange.org/

Search Strategies

Now let's look at some of the specific actions you'll need to take and some search strategies that you'll need to follow to ensure that you end up teaching at an international school that's right for you.

It used to be that almost all international school recruiting took place at hiring fairs that take place several times a year. However, so much of the recruiting is done now through the internet, and Skype has replaced the need for a face to face interview. Therefore, it is no longer the necessity it once was that a candidate for a teaching position attend a hiring fair.

Nevertheless, it can be very beneficial to sign up with one of the recruiting organizations that run the fairs, whether or not you decide to attend a fair on not. In addition to running these fairs, the recruiting organizations prequalify candidates and provide detailed listings for many of the international teaching positions that are available. Many of these listings can only be found through these organizations. In addition to this, even though the recruiting fairs seem to be getting closer and closer to obsolete, there are still many advantages to attending a hiring fair that will be discussed later in this guide.

Regardless of whether or not you decide to attend a recruiting fair, there are two main strategies that can be used to get hired by an international school. The first one we'll discuss focuses on the main part of the recruiting season, and the second one focuses on the later stage of the season. It is during the later stage of the recruiting season that less experienced teachers and those without any experience teaching internationally will have a better chance of getting hired.

The Winter Recruiting Strategy – Peak Season

The main recruiting season for international schools is in January and February. It is during this time period that the schools look to fill the bulk of their open teaching positions.

Once a teacher is employed by an international school, that teacher is expected to commit to either renewing or not renewing by December or early January for the next contractual period beginning the following autumn. This varies slightly from school to school, but international schools expect firm decisions to be made long in advance and have a signed contract in place before late January for teachers who will be staying on for the next school year.

So it is during January and February that the recruiting scene comes alive. Most of the major recruiting fairs happen during these two months, and the numbers of postings for jobs on the recruiting websites and on the schools' websites increase dramatically.

If you have worked at an international school before, if you have significant international experience, if you have IB experience and/or training, or if you teach in a shortage area (Math, Science, Special Education, and sometimes other subjects), you will be competitive during this prime period in recruitment, and you will be very likely to get multiple job offers if you pursue this search strategy. Teaching couples tend to do well during this period as well.

To pursue the winter strategy, contact the recruiting organizations that run the hiring fairs. Details about these organizations can be found in Part VI. By early October you are able to sign up with the agencies, at which point you get access to their databases which contain a wealth of information about schools, positions that are open, salaries, and benefits. If you think you might attend a fair, realize that most of the fairs have registration deadlines that fall well over a month before the fairs start. It is a good idea to look into these specific deadlines by September.

By December, you should identify several schools you're interested in and start sending out your resume. Do this whether or not the schools have posted vacancies in your subject area. Most international school recruiters conduct interviews through Skype before they head to the recruiting fairs, and if you have the skills and background that a school is looking for you may be offered a position before the January/February rush.

But don't be disheartened if you don't receive any replies. The schools, especially the more desirable ones, receive hundreds of email inquiries and don't have the time to respond to every teacher. Also, recruiters from these schools attend the recruiting fairs, and many of them prefer to hire candidates at these fairs.

Having made this initial contact prior to the fair paves the way for further discussion at the fair you attend. It also indicates that you are truly interested in that particular school.

Although hiring fairs can be costly to attend, they continue to be a great way to network. In addition to this, they offer many significant benefits to both recruiters and to teaching candidates.

Let's look at the hiring fairs and why they are beneficial to recruiters:

The hiring fairs separate out teachers who are serious about working at an international school from teachers who may be less serious. The process teachers go through and the expenses they incur to attend these fairs mean that there are very few candidates at hiring fairs who just want to find out information or maybe interview and then decide if international teaching is right for them.

The fairs give recruiters the opportunity to meet a large number of prescreened, qualified teachers in one place.

The normal protocol at career fairs is for schools to interview candidates for positions and offer contracts to suitable candidates on the spot. Candidates are given little time to consider the offers, often less than 24 hours. This means that recruiters can go to fairs with numerous vacancies and walk away with contracts signed by qualified candidates that they were able to interview face to face.

In the eyes of a recruiter, the hiring fair is a one-stop market where they can fill all or almost all of their open positions for the next school year.

All this means that if you get the chance to attend a recruiting fair, you will be given priority over the other teachers who are just emailing their resumes. Although it is never guaranteed that you will walk away from a hiring fair with a contract in hand, there are many benefits to attending one.

Now let's look at why hiring fairs are beneficial to candidates:

The stations at the fairs are staffed by the school administrators who are responsible for recruiting teachers. By simply walking up to one of the stations and starting a conversation, you are involved in an interview with a recruiter.

The recruiters have incentive to interview as many candidates as possible in the time that they have. Because of the ratio between schools and candidates and the number of interviews that can be conducted in a day, there are very few reasons why a school would decline to interview you for a vacancy, given that you are licensed to teach in that area and meet the school's most basic hiring requirements.

While candidates who email in their resumes have to wait until school administrators have time in their busy days to meet them through Skype, at hiring fairs recruiters have no tasks that are anywhere nearly as pressing as interviewing and hiring as many candidates as they have openings for.

By attending a hiring fair, you get the opportunity to show recruiters the person behind the resume and sell them on your qualifications and ability to teach their students face to face.

If you attend a hiring fair, you'll likely learn about schools and regions of the world that you may not have previously considered. At the fairs, there will be representatives from many great schools from great places around the world. The recruiters will be glad to explain to you the benefits of working for them.

Naturally there are drawbacks as well:

It is possible to attend a fair with several positions in mind and find most or even all of them filled before the fair you attend. In this case, you may need to be even more flexible than you thought you'd have to be and look elsewhere. If you don't, you'll likely end up leaving the fair without any job offers.

When jobs are offered at a fair, you will normally be offered a position either during or soon after your interview and expected to accept or decline almost immediately after you are offered the job (24 hours to decide is a luxury). Accepting the job means signing a two-year contract, or occasionally a one-year contract, with the school before you go home. At these fairs, there are very few exceptions to this process.

At fairs, the interview process and hiring process has a very intense and rushed feel to it. Big letdowns and difficult decisions are an integral part of the process. Prepare yourself mentally before you attend.

In order to attend a recruiting fair, you'll need to go through a screening process with the organization putting on the fair. You'll also need to pay the registration fee for the fair if there is one, pay for a flight to the city where the fair is being held, and most likely pay for a hotel room as well. In order to complete all of this, a teacher has to be serious and confident about the decision to teach at an international school.

To summarize the winter strategy:

Apply to the recruiting organization ad consider registering for a recruiting fair. Plan to register for a fair well before the deadline. By September you should know what the deadline is.

Research several schools that you would consider working at. Find their employment sections on their websites. Check for openings in your subject area. Learn as much about the schools as you possibly can and learn about the cities they are in. Research their salary and benefit packages. Information about the schools' salary and benefits packages are available in the databases of the recruiting organizations.

In December send your resume to schools you are interested in working at. Be prepared to be interviewed through Skype. Many schools like to do a significant part of their hiring before the fairs start.

Consider attending a hiring fair in January or February. The schools have paid large sums to attend these fairs and they know there will be many qualified candidates to interview at them.

From a school recruiter's perspective the hiring fairs are a great opportunity to take care of all or most of the hiring at once and not have to deal with much of it again. Because of this, these fairs are still a very good way to secure a position.

The Late Season Strategy: Round II of Recruiting and the Month of June

The winter fairs are attended by the most experienced and most highly qualified teachers. These teachers are actively sought by the schools recruiting at the winter fairs. Once the winter fairs are over, the pool of highly qualified and experienced international educators has diminished significantly. Therefore, the standards the schools adhere to for their hiring diminish as well. This means that after the winter fairs, the time is ideal for candidates who may be less qualified or less experienced.

When schools are unable to fill all of their positions during the winter stage of recruiting, they will then go back to the applications they received before the winter fairs and keep their postings active so that they can receive additional applications from teachers that are still looking for positions for the following fall. If you applied before the fairs, send additional emails to the schools you are still interested in from this category. It is even a good idea to attempt to contact recruiters by phone.

If you haven't yet sent off any applications, there will still be plenty of positions available after the winter fairs are over.

During this stage of recruiting, there are additional hiring fairs offered by the recruiting agencies, but all of these have much lower attendance than the winter fairs. During this time, most of the highly qualified teachers have already secured employment for the coming year, and most of the top tier schools and second tier schools have filled most of their positions and are confident that they can fill the rest without attending additional fairs.

The exception to this is the Summer Rush. This is the nickname for the final hiring fair held by Search Associates before the school year begins. ISS offers a similar fair around the same time. Details about both Search and ISS can be found in Part VI.

In the month of June many school heads find themselves in the uncomfortable position of not having filled all their open positions in the previous months. Fortunately for them, and for you, there are also recruiting fairs that take place in June. The June fairs can be described as the last desperation attempts by schools to fill positions that are still vacant, with just over a month to go before the classrooms are filled with students. Not more than 30 or 40 schools attend each June fair, but the ones who do are anxious to finally finish with their hiring, and generally only around 100 candidates attend these fairs looking for positions.

Most of the more desirable schools are able to fill their last openings in the early spring. But difficulties do arise, and positions open up all the time. If you are not very experienced or are having trouble getting hired, this may be your best opportunity. It is during this season and during the June recruiting fair that schools will greatly loosen their requirements. In June, a less qualified teacher who may not have any international experience may have a very good chance of getting hired by an international school.

If your qualifications are less than ideal, and you are open to work in parts of the world you may not have previously considered, Spring and the month of

June might be the best time for you to seek employment.

Once June ends, the schools close for the summer, and their recruiters take their well-deserved vacations. If a position isn't filled by the end of June, there is still work to be done, so recruiters will do just about anything, including accepting candidates who fall well below their usual standards to avoid continuing recruiting into the summer or starting in the Fall short-staffed.

In addition to this recruitment pattern, there are some schools that do very little recruiting during the normal peak season of January and February. These schools are often very competitive to get hired at. Also they tend to be schools that are more able to hire expat locals. If a school you're interested in has no postings for positions during January and February, continue checking for openings with them in March and April. Schools in popular vacation spots such as Costa Rica fall into this category as do some of the top schools in Western Europe.

Which Strategy Should You Use?

It is reasonable for a prospective international school teacher to employ both the January/February and the late season strategies. The question is where should you focus your time, energy, and money? Recruiting fairs are expensive to attend, and a job search is always time consuming. The answer depends on how qualified you are to work in an international school.

The Winter Strategy

If you have taught internationally before, if you have significant international experience, if you have IB experience or training, or if you teach in a shortage area, and you feel that you will be a strong candidate, you should follow these steps.

In December, begin applying to schools in response to jobs that are posted and also to schools that have not posted jobs but you are interested in working at. Send a copy of your resume and a cover letter tailored to each school you are interested in applying to.

If you haven't been offered a job, attend the earliest recruiting fair possible in late January or early February. At the recruiting fairs, schools will generally make offers to the first qualified candidate that they meet. There are several recruiting fairs in a short period of time, and schools send their recruiters to as many fairs as they can fit into their schedules. Therefore there will be more jobs available at the earliest fair than there will be at the latest fair, assuming that the same number of schools attend both. Some schools might add positions as the month goes on, but this is fairly rare. Most of the recruiting that takes place at the fairs is decided before the first fair starts. So if you are attending the last fair in February, you are more likely to find that the top three schools on your list have all filled their openings, before you can even ask the recruiters about them. The one benefit to attending later fairs is that the school recruiters that haven't yet filled positions will become more willing to lower their standards and accept a candidate who might be less qualified than they would otherwise like to hire. In general, if you are well qualified, you're better off attending the earliest fair possible to avoid the disappointment of having schools that you were anxious to work at not even meet with you, because they filled your position at a previous fair.

Follow up on all your contacts. Send handwritten thank you notes to recruiters you meet in person, and send emails thanking recruiters who interview you through Skype. It isn't a bad idea to be conversational and let the recruiters you met with know what's happening with your job search. You never know what can come of building a contact this way: maybe a future position at the school, or maybe a referral to another school. Work hard to build a set of contacts, even before your first job at an international school.

Over the next few months, continue reviewing postings and websites of schools you are interested in. Apply for jobs that come up. Some teachers sign or renew contracts and then for various reasons break these contracts later in the year. Look for these opportunities to apply and reapply for positions.

Consider attending one of the June recruiting fairs. Fewer schools attend this one, and far fewer positions are offered, but recruiters are very anxious to fill their open positions before summer break starts. If you're not too picky about where you'll work, the June fair offers an excellent opportunity to secure a position.

Use the first few months of the school year to improve your resume and your qualifications. Incorporate what you've learned in your search to strengthen your chances of being hired in the next recruiting wave.

Repeat steps one and two. If you don't leave the February fair with a signed contract, there must be something wrong. Maybe you're being too selective about schools or regions. Maybe there are factors that are making recruiters less willing to hire you. You need to find out what the problem is. Can you change your circumstances to make yourself a more attractive candidate?

The Late Season Strategy

If you are a teacher who hasn't worked at an international school before, if you don't have other significant international experience, if you don't have IB experience or training, if you don't teach in a shortage area, or if you would just like to start your job search at a time when the competition won't be as significant, you should follow these steps.

In late February, begin looking through job postings and contacting schools you're interested in working for, whether you find jobs posted or not. Send a copy of your resume and a cover letter tailored to each school you are interested in applying to. It is very important that you do not just send the same generic letter to each school. Recruiters can spot these immediately and will put your application at the bottom of the pile if you do. Research the school you are applying to. In your letter mention something you've discovered about the school, along with how you can contribute to specific programs or initiatives that the school is publicizing on their website or in articles you've read.

If you haven't been offered a job by late April, sign up for a June recruiting fair. Attend the fair in your interview attire and be prepared to convince recruiters there is no reason that they should consider any candidates other than you. Make some contacts. Get some business cards. When you contact these same recruiters in the future, they will know you already and will be more likely to hire you.

If you find yourself back at your old school in September, work on improving your resume. You have now met a number of school recruiters and probably have a much better idea of what they're looking for. Consider what you have learned from your experience so far. If you were unfamiliar with a set of skills or a type of training that the recruiters were stressing, read up on it. Maybe take an online course to familiarize yourself with it. There is not much recruiting that goes on from September through January, but if you are not employed, or if you are able to leave your job on good terms with little notice, there will be jobs available that begin after the school year has started. It is never easy for a teacher to start teaching after the school year has begun, but this may be your chance to get your foot in the door and start your career in international teaching.

In December start sending your resume to schools again. Focus on the schools you have already expressed interest in and touch base with those you have already had contact with. Your persistence may pay off. Recruiters who have already met you and who have a good impression of you may prefer hiring you over a stranger.

Consider attending a recruiting fair in January or February. These are the main recruiting fairs, and your familiarity with the recruiting process will give you an advantage.

Continue contacting school recruiters after the fairs. Look to get a position at one of the schools that was unable to fill its requirements at the fairs.

If you still have not secured a position, repeat step one, and ask the school recruiters, especially the ones you have already made contact with what it would take for you to get hired. By this time, after a year of searching, with teaching certification and at least a couple of years of quality experience you should have secured a job. But international teaching isn't for everyone. If you are being too selective about where you go, or if you are not sure this is the right path for you to take, this might be getting in the way of your job search.

Accepting a Job

Regardless of which strategy you use, you're very likely to be offered a job or multiple jobs if you're persistent and you begin following either of these strategies.

Once you're offered a position with a school, make sure that if you decide to accept the job, your decision is based on what you know about the school and where you'll be moving to. To avoid spending two years working at a school where you'd rather not be, do your research as early as possible about schools and countries you're interested in.

It's important that you have as much information as possible regarding the position you're about to enter into. You'll definitely be better off if you've done enough research to make your decision before you're asked to decide on the spot whether or not you'll be working for a particular school for the next two years.

Contact current teachers. When you do, try to go beyond the list of teachers that the school administrators hand you when they interview you or offer you a job. Ask how you would be able to get in touch with teachers who might not be on the list of teachers provided to you by the school. If you search Facebook with the name of a school you're interested in, you'll probably come up with a list of current and former teachers that you can contact.

Be wary of a school that is unwilling to let you contact its teachers. Contact a few teachers and try to get confidential replies. Do some research on the internet. Read the school reviews on *International Schools Review* (www.internationalschoolsreview.com). This website is discussed further in Part VI, but it's important to note here that anonymous reviews, such as the ones posted at this site, are not the most trustworthy. Learn as much as possible about the schools you're applying to. Research the city that you'll be moving to. How's the weather? How's the food?

If you're offered a job on the spot by a school that you weren't previously considering, it might be difficult to do as much research as you would like. In this case, you'll have to learn as much as you can and then make a decision. Even if you're only given 24 hours, you'll probably have enough time to contact a few teachers by phone. It's enough time to learn about the city you'll be moving to. It's enough time to read a little bit about the school.

Avoid signing any contract without taking at least a few hours to think and do some final research.

Recruiters have been known, particularly at hiring fairs, to pressure teachers to sign contracts on the spot, but if you insist you should be able to negotiate for a period of at least a few hours (hopefully 24 hours) to make your decision.

Make sure that you have enough information to make the right decision, so that you're confident about where you'll teach for the next two years, and you'll be less likely to run into problems later on.

Problems That You Might Run into When You're Teaching Abroad

As is the case with any job, the person hired does not always work out. People are fired and people quit jobs for a variety of reasons. International schools are no different. Not all teachers that are hired work out and complete their contracts. However, unlike some jobs where a new employee can often be found quite readily, international schools need to invest a great deal of time, money, and resources to recruit teachers from abroad and even more to bring teachers in from abroad, process their work permits, and set them up in apartments. It is because of this that international schools generally lock their teachers in with two year contracts. (As was mentioned earlier, two years is standard, while a few schools offer one year contracts.). This limits your ability to voluntarily leave, and it also limits your employer's ability to replace you.

If you are in a job at an international school and things aren't going well, usually the best thing to do is wait until the end of your contract and then move on, rather than break your contract. Breaking a contract can have serious consequences. If you do so without the written approval of your school, it is unlikely that you will be able to register with any of the international school recruiting agencies for at least a few years. Also school administrators do communicate with one another, and the word that you have broken a contract can spread and, as was pointed out earlier, get in the way of your getting hired by another international school.

If for some reason it just isn't possible for you to complete your contract, it is important to be open and honest with management about your situation. You may be let out of your contract if you use this approach. But remember, in the eyes of school administrators, if you sign a two year contract, you are expected to fulfill the terms of it and stay for the entire two years. Often teachers are not given consent to break contracts, even if they have what they consider valid reasons.

Part IV

Benefits and Salaries

Benefits

Housing

Whether or not a school provides housing or a housing allowance makes a very big difference financially, so make sure that this is one of the first things you look for when reviewing packages offered by schools. A housing allowance or employee housing is provided in addition to the salary you are paid by the vast majority of international schools, with the exception of most Western European schools and a few others.

If a school provides a housing allowance instead of an apartment, be sure you ask for details on how much of the actual cost of housing the allowance will cover. It won't always cover all of your rent.

If your school has special apartments for teachers, be sure you get details on these as well. If you're offered housing near school or on the school's premises it's good to know if your apartment will be near student housing? If your job is at a boarding school, will your duties extend to watching the students after school hours? Will you have the privacy you'd like?

If you are offered a job in a big city, the housing might be on the outskirts of the city and make the city inaccessible, except on weekends. Make sure you're comfortable with the housing arrangements before you sign your contract.

In general, schools in Western Europe, as well as a few other schools internationally, do not provide housing or an allowance. The lack of housing will significantly lower your total income, especially in the high-rent cities of Western Europe.

Whether or not you school provides you with housing and whether you're provided with an apartment or an allowance can make a big difference. Therefore you should focus your attention on it when you're considering schools.

Health Insurance

Schools offer a wide range of health insurance programs. Some plans include dental and vision, and will likely be far superior to your domestic policy. Most will offer less. Some schools offer only basic insurance through a contract with a local hospital. If you're unhappy with the adequacy of the school's policy, it is possible to contract with a provider of international insurance. One of the best known of these is Bupa (www.bupa.com). Be aware that preexisting conditions are less likely to be covered internationally than they are by United States based insurance companies, and exclusions from coverage might go beyond what you're used to.

Airfares

It is standard for schools to provide airfare to the school at the beginning of the contract and home at the end of the contract. Some schools offer airfare for you and your dependents, some for only you. Some schools offer annual airfare, while others stick to offering it at the beginning and end of each two year contract. Calculate what you will pay for your annual trips home and consider this along with income when you are comparing schools.

Tuition for Dependent Children

Here you'll find a wide variety of offerings. Some schools offer free tuition for one or more children while some only offer a discount. Most have a limit on the number of dependents teachers can send to the school without paying full tuition. Generally free or reduced tuition is limited to one child per teacher employed by the school.

Be sure to check if free or reduced tuition is taxed. You may end up paying a significant portion of the value of the tuition to the government if this is the case.

Assistance with Visas

Your school should handle all the paperwork associated with processing your work visa. This is generally the case, but international school teachers have occasionally had to wait in lines at immigration offices.

Taxes

There are many schools that offer tax free salaries. Very often the schools that offer these are just paying the local taxes and not reporting these taxes to teachers. The US government does have tax treaties with many countries, and certain educators are covered in these tax treaties. Nevertheless, international school teachers are not covered by tax treaties.

Be sure you check with the school and do some research on the local tax situation before accepting a contract if the tax issue hasn't been made completely clear. Tax rates can vary and can significantly cut into your salary. Tax rates can also change from year to year. For example, in 2012 China raised the tax rate it will charge international school teachers. Some schools in

China are paying the additional expense and others are not. If you're offered a contract to teach in China or anywhere else, be sure you clarify whether the salary you are quoted is a net or gross salary, and find out exactly how much you will be taxed.

As of 2013, US citizens are exempt from US taxes on income up to $97,600, as long as they are physically present and a resident of a foreign country for 330 days during a 12 month period. Citizens of other countries are not required to pay taxes on income earned abroad.

Salaries at International Schools

Specific information about salary packages at international schools are often kept relatively quiet. It can be difficult to find information on salaries published anywhere unless you are registered as actively searching for employment with Search Associates, ISS or one of the other recruiting agencies. This is one of the biggest benefits of registering with a recruiting agency. However, once you inform the agency that you have accepted a position, your access to their database will be removed along with all their information about salaries.

For those who don't have this access, a useful bit of information about salary ranges is that they are often defined somewhat by the region or by the country the school is in. The regional profiles in the *Where Will You Go* section in Part I will give you some idea. Schools in some regions can be expected to pay better than schools in others, but there will also be variation in salaries among schools within a country.

Many factors go into the salary ranges at international schools. The ease the schools have in recruiting teachers is one factor that contributes to what schools are willing to pay. Costa Rican schools, for example, have no trouble recruiting teachers, and the salaries are quite low. Pakistani schools, with the current political situation there, have more trouble, and the salaries there are quite high. Schools that are highly rated academically aim to recruit the best teachers in their fields, and they often pay high salaries relative to their locations.

In addition to salary you'll also need to consider the cost of living in the country you are thinking of moving to. A moderate salary in Vietnam will likely go much further than a high salary in France, especially since schools in France generally do not provide housing, while those in Vietnam generally do.

Part V

Relationship Status and How it Can Affect Your Job Search

Unlike traditional job searches, international schools will need to know far more about your personal life than you are probably used to sharing with prospective employers. In addition to this, there are personal factors that can greatly impact your chances of getting hired by an international school. The most significant one is relationship status.

Relationship Status

Uncomfortable as it may be, your relationship status will be an issue when it comes to being hired as a teacher at an international school. Some schools prefer single teachers, most prefer to hire teaching couples and prioritize them over all others, and many schools do not like to hire teachers with a non-teaching spouse or partner.

Single Teachers

This is a very good category you can find yourself in when you're searching for an international teaching job. Just about all schools, with the exception of some of the Saudi Arabian schools that will only hire married couples, will consider you.

Teaching Couples

If you and your spouse or significant other are both teachers, you will very likely have an advantage. Most schools tend to favor teaching couples over single teachers when they are able to find a couple that fills two separate vacancies. Processing visas is easier, and it's less costly and time-consuming to find housing for a couple than for two single teachers living separately. The one problem with teaching couples is that a school will have to have openings in both teachers' subjects. Some schools actually set aside openings in primary school to save them for teaching couples where one teacher is a secondary teacher in a shortage area while the other one works in primary.

Schools that have openings in positions, that both you and your spouse are well qualified for, will likely give you special consideration and make an effort to find a way to fit you in. This applies to married couples, unmarried couples, and even, for the most part, gay couples. Whether a school will consider an unmarried couple or a gay couple depends somewhat on the acceptance of these ways of life in the country where the school is. However, you may be surprised; there are even schools in what you might think of as very conservative countries that will hire unmarried teaching couples and gay teaching couples. Check with the individual schools and with the organization that runs the recruiting fair you plan on attending regarding your individual situation.

Teachers with a Non-Teaching Spouse

Being in this position will limit the number of opportunities you have available. Some schools will not hire teachers who plan on moving with their non-teaching spouse, except as a last resort. This has a lot to do with the immigration laws in the country. Countries like Brazil make it nearly impossible for the spouse of a sponsored teacher to work legally in the country.

Schools will hesitate to hire you with a non-teaching spouse, if there's any reason to worry that supporting both you and your spouse on one salary will be a burden. They may also worry that having your spouse in a foreign country without working during the day will create a strain on your relationship and reduce your effectiveness as a teacher or make you less likely to complete your contract.

If you plan on seeking employment with a non-teaching spouse, make this clear to the schools to which you are applying. For some schools, considering you will not be an option.

In this case, your spouse might want to consider also getting certified to teach since teaching couples have far more success finding employment.

Children

Generally if a teacher has more than one dependent, or if a teaching couple has more than two dependents, this will make a job search more difficult. If you have children, check with individual schools regarding their policies on hiring teachers with children.

Also be sure you check on whether or not your children will be able to attend the school and if they are will you have to pay tuition for them to do so?

Pet Ownership

It is not a problem to bring your pets into some countries, and it is very difficult in others. Regardless, you should expect to have your pets examined by a veterinarian before your trip. PetTravel.com (www.pettravel.com) has country specific information about countries you may move to with pets, as well as general information about traveling internationally with them.

Part VI

Websites, Recruiting Agencies, and Other Resources for International School Teaching Candidates

Essential Websites

When you decide to seriously begin your search, there are some websites that you should be checking regularly for job postings and other updated information. Some of these charge fees which are generally well worth the price.

Included in this category should be the websites of all the schools you're interested in. Be sure to identify them as early as possible and check them regularly for updates in their job postings.

The general websites you'll need to check regularly are:

Times Educational Supplement (TES)

This is the educational supplement to the Times of London, and it is free online. The primary function of the section is to provide information and listings for UK based jobs, but in the search link there is a category for international teaching jobs that is quite extensive.

Overall this is probably the top search site for international teaching positions, but since it is UK focused, the number of opportunities for teachers who do not have experience teaching the British curriculum is somewhat limited, although many schools that post here do not require this background. Be sure you check the TES listings regularly as new job openings are posted here daily, especially during the winter months.

The job search link for TES is:

http://www.tes.co.uk/jobsHub.aspx?navcode=6

International Schools Review (ISR)

ISR provides essential information about international schools that is written anonymously, but it often provides reviews that are quite negative. ISR is the place to look if you want to find out the potential problems that exist at international schools you are considering applying to. ISR specializes in reviews of international schools that are written by teachers. Any registered member of ISR can post reviews.

If you take the negative reviews on this site as an accurate depiction of what it's like to work at an international school, you'll quickly decide that this is not the career for you. However, it should be clear to a discerning observer that the bulk of the negative reviews on this site are written by disgruntled teachers. A side effect of the resource that is offered by ISR is that teachers who have a grudge against a school they worked at are able to post a negative review about that school. On the other hand, some of the positive reviews appear to be written by school administrators.

When reading reviews on ISR, a good rule of thumb is to give more credence to negative comments when multiple reviews mention that the school lost its accreditation, or that the principal left for good in the middle of the night, than you do to reviews that vaguely talk about power hungry administrators. Also consider a positive review to be more credible when it gives a balanced report that talks about positive and negative factors of working at the school, than when it cites statistics and paints a glowing picture of a school that sounds too good to be true.

Reading between the lines of the reviews on ISR can provide valuable information about the schools and the cities you are thinking of working in. In addition to reading up on what has been said about a school on ISR, it is good to do some due diligence of your own. Make sure that you have really looked into the school and the city where you'll be spending the next two years before you sign a contract that commits you to do so.

In addition to the reviews that subscribers to ISR are able to read, ISR forums are indispensable as well. They're constantly reviewed by experienced international school teachers who are able to quickly answer even the most obscure questions about all topics regarding international schools.

ISR is highly recommended. A teacher searching for a job at an international school is sure to find useful information on this site. At this time, the cost to join ISR is $29 per year, but it is free to sign up for the forums.

The website for ISR is:

www.internationalschoolsreview.com

The International Educator (TIE)

TIE is a great source of information about who's hiring at international schools. It also provides information about a number of issues that are important to international school teachers and prospective teachers, from what it takes to become an international school teacher to information about health insurance.

The TIE newspaper is published quarterly and it contains many informative articles on all aspects of international education. TIE even has a *News from Schools* section in their publication. Look there for schools you may be interested in, and read about them. Being able to talk about what's happening at the school you're applying to will put you at an advantage. One of TIE's strongest points is its online job listings that are updated daily and include listings from many well-known international schools.

When searching for a position, especially during the recruiting season, TIE can give you a pretty good idea of which schools are hiring teachers in your subject and which schools are not. TIE also will give you some information about the salary and benefits packages that are offered by the schools in their listings.

The cost to subscribe to TIE is $39 per year for access to the website and to the online version of the quarterly newspaper ($49 if you opt to receive the print version of TIE's newspaper).

The website for TIE is:

http://www.tieonline.com/

Recruiting Agencies and Hiring Fairs

Registration with a Recruiting Agency

Recruiting agencies have standards to ensure that the teachers registering with them and attending their hiring fairs are qualified to work for international schools. This prescreening makes the jobs of the school recruiters who work with these agencies much easier.

In order to attend a recruiting fair you'll need to have a valid teaching license, experience, and letters of recommendation from your supervisors. You'll be required to fill out a detailed application and you may even be required to have your references submit confidential recommendations on your behalf.

In order to finalize your registration with a recruiting agency, you'll also need to sign a contract that, in addition to other things, states that you guarantee you won't break any teaching contract you enter into and that, if you do so, you'll face a financial penalty. As was mentioned earlier, it is very important that you are sure that you are ready to teach abroad before entering into a contract to do so.

Attending a Hiring Fair

Remember many teachers get hired by international schools without attending hiring fairs, and the fairs are costly. Even the free fairs require that you sign up with a recruiting agency and pay for your trip to the fair's location. Nevertheless, there are many benefits to attending these fairs

In order to attend a hiring fair you'll need to:

Register with the recruiting agency that's holding the fair.

Register for the fair in advance. Check with the recruiting agency regarding the deadline, but because you'll likely need confidential recommendations, three or four months before the fair is held is not too soon to start the process.

Again, the busiest recruiting fairs are in February. Most of the top-tier and second-tier schools attend these fairs. Also most of the highly qualified and experienced international school teachers, who are looking for jobs, attend these fairs. Later in the season there are better opportunities to secure good jobs with less powerful qualifications than you would need at the fairs in January and February.

If you attend a June recruiting fair, you will be dealing with a lot less competition and with recruiters who are anxious to hire. You will, however, have fewer choices. Fewer schools recruit and, if you accept a job, it may be in a region of the world where you never expected to work. On the bright side, however, for teachers new to international education, this is a good way to break into the field.

When you pay the fees to sign up with a recruiting agency, you are paying for access to their database, which contains detailed information about many schools that includes their salary ranges and benefits packages. You are also paying for the privilege to attend fairs hosted by that agency.

There are no guarantees that by signing up with one of these agencies you will be placed. People from the recruiting agencies will likely give you advice about which fairs to attend, but making connections with schools and getting the job is up to you. Be sure to brush up on your interviewing skills before attending a fair. You'll need to be able to concisely describe your qualifications, and be ready to talk in depth about your subject and your teaching techniques.

Schools pay a placement fee to the recruiting agency when they hire teachers through use of its database or through attendance at a fair, and it is primarily the schools that the agencies are there to serve. Nevertheless, make regular contact with the people running the fair you plan on attending, and ask for advice when needed.

The Recruiting Agencies

The big three of the international school recruiting agencies are Search Associates, ISS, and the University of Northern Iowa. All three of these will give you access to a large number of job openings. They will provide you with detailed information about the schools, what they offer and what they require. They work with a large variety of schools from the best out there to ones that are not as great to work at. If you are offered a job through any of the recruiting agencies, be sure you don't neglect to research the school thoroughly. Just because you get a job through a reputable agency doesn't mean you'll have a great experience at the school you work at.

Search Associates

This is the best known recruiting agency for international schools and the largest. Search works without about 600 schools from around the world. When you sign up with Search Associates, you will be assigned a representative to advise you and direct you to which fairs and which schools are most appropriate for you based on your qualifications. Search holds around ten fairs per year internationally.

In order to take part in Search Associates fairs, you'll need to sign up online with Search. You'll pay $225 to sign up for a three year period or until you are placed with a school. This includes an invitation to one fair. Additional fairs are available for $75 per fair.

The Search Associates website is:

www.searchassociates.com

International Schools Services (ISS)

ISS holds five recruiting fairs each year internationally. ISS is smaller than Search and, in general, a little more selective about the schools it recruits for. For $195 you can register with ISS for two years. Once you've been accepted by ISS and paid this fee, you'll then be able to sign up for ISS fairs, which are free to attend. ISS is more selective than Search. ISS only accepts experienced teachers and only recruits for schools that are established and highly regarded. This can be advantageous to teachers who already have a few years of experience. Registration opens around the beginning of September, so if you're considering attending fairs during the prime recruiting season in the Winter, it is best to be signed up by October.

The ISS website is:

www.iss.edu/education-careers

University of Northern Iowa Overseas Placement Service

Compared to Search Associates and ISS, the University of Northern Iowa Overseas Placement Service is low budget and no-frills. Its sole focus is on one recruiting fair held once per year. It is also inexpensive compared to other recruiting agencies. It charges a flat rate of $150. You will even receive a discount if you register early enough (see their website for details). It is a good choice, if you are looking for a fair during the prime recruiting season of early February, although the weather in Iowa is certainly not at its best in February. The fair is large, and you'll need to make an effort to get noticed by the schools you are targeting. There are many schools and many candidates at this fair. Strong credentials and experience will distinguish you from the other candidates here, but there are plenty of opportunities for newer and less experienced teachers as well.

The UNI Overseas Recruiting website is:

www.uni.edu/placement/overseas

In addition to the big three, there are a few other recruiting agencies that you might want to consider depending on what you're looking for.

The Association of American Schools in South America (AASSA)

For teachers interested in working in the Caribbean or any part of Latin America, not just South America, despite the name, AASSA holds its annual fair in late November or early December in Atlanta, Georgia. Many Latin American schools run their school year from January through December. Hence the earlier than normal date for this fair. The registration fee is $110 to attend the fair.

The AASSA website is:

www.aassa.com

Council of International Schools (CIS)

CIS holds an annual fair in London, UK. This is a non-profit organization that doesn't charge teachers for fairs. CIS is UK centric and ideal for UK based teachers who are looking to teach internationally.

CIS also has an extensive directory of schools on their website.

The CIS website is:

www.cois.org

Teachers' Overseas Recruiting Fair (TORF)

TORF is Canada's premier recruiting fair. It is run by Queen's University. It's held in late January and attracts a good number of quality international schools. The fee to register for it is $125.

The TORF website is:

http://educ.queensu.ca/services/careers/international/torf.html

Part VII

Final Words and a Directory of Some Well Known International Schools

Final Words

Before you begin your search for a job teaching abroad make sure this is the right decision. Once you do, define yourself as a candidate, and create a detailed strategy that should include extensive contact with recruiters, regular review of essential websites, and perhaps a trip to a hiring fair. Research is necessary every step of the way. Moving abroad to teach is a major decision.

Once you move abroad, take the time to travel, enjoy the city you live in, and really experience the culture. Teaching is intense work, so it may take some effort to enjoy your new home. Make sure you do all the things that tourists do and locals don't do. See the Great Wall if you're in China, the Eifel Tower if you're in France, or the Pyramids if you're in Egypt. Time will fly by once you're living abroad and it will be too easy to miss out on all the wonders your new home has to offer unless you make an effort not to.

Some of the Better-Known International Schools

This is by no means an all inclusive list of international schools, but most of these schools are well known and considered desirable places to work for teachers looking for positions internationally. Most of them also have good reputations, high salaries, or a combination of both.

Perhaps this can serve as a guide and help you start or move along with your job search. Look into some of the schools listed. Review their mission statements. Look for their employment information. Maybe you'll be inspired to begin your search with one of them.

Angola

Luanda International School - www.lisluanda.com

Argentina

Lincoln American International School - www.lincoln.edu.ar

Austria

American International School Vienna - www.ais.at

Danube International School - www.danubeschool.at

Vienna International School - www.vis.ac.at

Belgium

British School of Brussels - www.britishschool.be

International Schools Brussels - www.isb.be/index.cfm

Brazil

Graded - www.graded.br

Chile

Nido de Aguilar - www.nido.cl

China

Beijing International School BISS - www.biss.com.cn

International School of Beijing - www.isb.bj.edu.cn

British International School Shanghai - www.bisshanghai.com

Shanghai American School - www.saschina.org

Shanghai Community International - www.scischina.org

Czech Republic

International School of Prague - www.isp.cz

Denmark

Copenhagen International School - www.cis-edu.dk

Egypt

Cairo American College - www.cacegypt.org

Modern English School, Cairo - www.mescairo.com

New Cairo British International School - www.ncbis.org

Schutz American School - www.schutzschool.org.eg

Finland

International School of Helsinki - www.ish.edu.hel.fi

France

American School of Paris - www.asparis.org

International School of Paris - www.isparis.edu

Germany

Berlin International School - www.berlin-international-school.de

Berlin Metropolitan School - www.berlinmetropolitanschool.com

Cologne International School - www.is-cologne.de

John F. Kennedy School, Berlin - www.jfks.de

Greece

American Community Schools Athens - www.acs.gr

Holland

American International School.Rotterdam - www.aisr.nl

American School of the Hague - www.ash.nl

International School of the Hague - www.ishthehague.nl

Hong Kong

American International School - www.ais.edu.hk

Hong Kong International School - www.hkis.edu.hk

Hungary

American International School of Budapest - www.aisb.hu

British International School of Budapest - www.bisb.hu

India

American Embassy School Delhi - aes.ac.in//splash.php

American School Bombay - www.asbindia.org

International School Bangalore - site.tisb.org

Indonesia

Bali International School- www.baliinternationalschool.com

British International School Jakarta - www.bis.or.id

Jarkata International School - www.jisedu.or.id

North Jakarta International School - www.njis.org

Italy

American Overseas School Rome - www.aosr.org

American School of Milan - www.asmilan.org

International School Milan - www.ism-ac.it

Japan

American School in Japan - community.asij.ac.jp/Page.aspx?&srcid=-2

Kyoto International School - www.kyotointernationalschool.org

Tokyo International School - www.tokyois.com

Yokohama International School - www.yis.ac.jp

Kenya

International School of Kenya - www.isk.ac.ke

Korea

Asia Pacific International School - www.apis.seoul.kr

Seoul Foreign School - www.seoulforeign.org

Seoul International School - www.siskorea.org

Luxembourg

International School Luxembourg - www.islux.lu

Malaysia

International School of Kuala Lumpur - www.iskl.edu.my/index_content.php

Monaco

International School of Monaco - www.ismonaco.org

Morocco

American School of Marrakesh - www.asm.ac.ma

Mozambique

American International School - www.aism-moz.com

Myanmar

International School of Myanmar - www.ismyanmar.com

Norway

Trondheim International School - this.no

Philippines

International School Manila - www.ismanila.org

Poland

American School of Warsaw - www.aswarsaw.org

Romania

American International School Bucharest - www.aisb.ro

British School Romania - www.britishschool.ro

Russia

Anglo-American School Moscow - www.aas.ru

Anglo-Amer. School St. Petersburg - www.aas.ru/stpetersburg.cfm

British International School Moscow - www.bismoscow.com

Senegal

International School of Dakar - www.isdakar.org

Singapore

Chinese International School - www.cnis.edu.sg

International School Singapore - www.iss.edu.sg

Singapore American School - www.sas.edu.sg

South Africa

American International School Cape Town - www.aisct.org

Spain

International School Madrid - www.icsmadrid.org

Switzerland

The American School in Switzerland - switzerland.tasis.com

International School Berne - www.isberne.ch

International School Geneva - -Campus des Nations - www.ecolint.ch

International School Lausanne - www.isl.ch

John F Kennedy International School - www.jfk.ch

Le Rosey - www.rosey.ch

Zurich International School - www.zis.ch

Syria

Damascus Community School - www.dcssyria.org

Taiwan

Taipei American School - www.tas.edu.tw

Taipei European School Taipei - www.taipeieuropeanschool.com

Thailand

American School of Bangkok - www.asb.ac.th

Bangkok Patana School - www.patana.ac.th

International School Bangkok - www.isb.ac.th

Turkey

Istanbul International Community - www.iics.k12.tr

United Arab Emirates

American School of Dubai - www.asdubai.org

British International School, Abu Dhabi - www.bisabudhabi.com

Dubai International Academy - www.diadubai.com

Uruguay

Uruguayan American School - www.uas.edu.uy

Venezuela

Escuela Campo Alegre - www.ecak12.com

Vietnam

British International School - www.bisvietnam.com

International School Ho Chi Minh City - www.ishcmc.com

Saigon South International - www.ssis.edu.vn

United Nations International School, Hanoi - www.unishanoi.org

www.ingramcontent.com/pod-product-compliance
Lightning Source LLC
Chambersburg PA
CBHW051725170526
45167CB00002B/807